Tia's Journey to Faith

A True Story About a Lost Dog

Rose Reese

DEDICATION

I dedicate this book to my Heavenly Father who showed me, through the love of a little black dog, that life is about believing in miracles.

Holding on is not what makes us strong, sometimes it is about letting go.

ACKNOWLEDGEMENTS

Where do you begin when it comes time to thank everyone? There were so many people all over the world. I could fill another book with the names of those who helped us. I still have people stop me and tell me how much they prayed for both of us during this trying time.

I would like to start out by thanking my amazing husband Randy Reese, he was there to support me through the tough times and has been my rock when I felt all was impossible. He gave me hope and encouraged me to be strong and keep believing, even when it came time to write this book.

Jeff Reese, my son, who didn't hesitate to come up when called to help look for Tia. Also for spending many hours in the pouring rain accompanying Sam and Brie (the tracker dog). David Reese, my son, who helped with the search, Kelli Reese, my daughter-in-law and grandchildren for being there for me.

Betty Ann my sister, who I know I can always count on for being a prayer warrior and Bill my brother-in-law, who helped with the search. Then there's Butchie Sofranko, my sister-in-law, for encouraging me to call Roseann.

Debbie Bower, a very good friend and animal communicator who I can always rely on for her expertise and caring nature.

Bonnie Lazorick, your friendship means so very much. Thank you for making the initial flyers for you and Donna to distribute and for always being there.

Donna Kattner, you are the best, I can't thank you enough for always being there. Your support and continued support with our lengthy phone calls listening to my fears and challenges will never be forgotten. Also your assistance with Pure Gold Trackers, many thanks.

Becky Marzen, who came to my aid and spent many days in the search also providing knowledge of what to do next.

Roseann Turek, a local medium, for taking the time to come up and lead a group of my family and friends on the search.

Marsha Wallace, Debbie Gigliotti, Heidi Seiwell and Tonya Middaugh, who spent many hours calling veterinarians, rescues, shelters, etc, thank you so very much.

Cyndi Simmons, who helped by stuffing newspapers and delivering to local homes.

Tom Connors, who with his help made the local television interview a reality.

Susie Yaich, who with her help made the newspaper article a reality.

Rose Strubinger, Milans Printing, and Peggy Dart, who revised and made new flyers for our continued search.

James Van Praagh and Samantha Khury for giving me hope and direction.

Father James Torpey for his encouraging words and for providing me with the blessed candle and bible.

Judy Nederostek for continuing to help me replenish the candles.

Bonnie Mastromatto for giving me Faith to love.

Jacki Delong, Lisa Bonaldi, and Lisa Fauzio, who I have never met in person but have become lifelong friends and who continue to support me.

Donna Kattner, Betty Ann Flyte, Pennie Leibensperger Kern, Mary Ellen Hawk, Daniel Lisella, Mary Bodin, Jacqui Petch and Bonnie Lazorick for reviewing my story before it was sent to the editor.

Kate McGahan, writer and editor, who believed in me and with her expertise and guidance made this book a reality. Thank you for always being there.

For all my family and friends for their support and prayers; I will be forever grateful.

Tia's Journey to Faith

I am a firm believer that God has a purpose for everyone. Not only people but our pets too. This is a story about a little black dog named Tia. She came to live with us 16 years ago. A friend's dog was due to have puppies. It was believed she was only going to have two, but when the time came, to my friend's surprise, three puppies were born on December 22, 2008. She called me and asked if I would be interested in giving one of them a good home. We already had two dogs, Mickey and Molly, but we decided she would come live with us. I convinced my husband by stating she would actually be my granddaughter's dog, but live with us because she couldn't have a dog where she lived. Tia was a normal puppy and throughout the years gave us much joy and laughter. She was very intelligent but also had a mind of her own, very independent. She was still very much alert on her 15th birthday. Within a few months after that however, I noticed her hearing and eyesight were starting to decline. She also seemed to be starting with some dementia. She was still eating (although very picky) and drinking. Her favorite food was spaghetti and homemade chicken pot pie. She could still go up and down the stairs, but I felt safer carrying her.

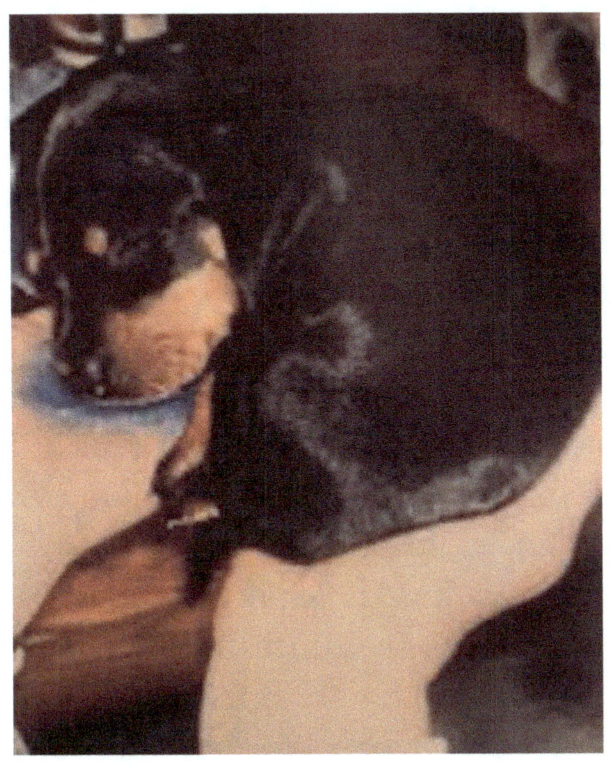

In June I had foot surgery which had me non-weight bearing for two months. Family and friends came to help get Tia in and out. We have a completely fenced-in backyard so there were times she would also take herself out to walk around. I was so happy she could do this and I knew she would be safe.

Then, on July 30th she actually chased a rabbit when my husband had her out. We laughed stating she still had spunk. Then, on July 31st at 6 pm her life and mine changed forever. My husband and I were getting ready to go to my grandson's baseball game. I took Tia and the other two dogs outside. I thought I'd let her walk around with them before bringing them inside so we could leave. When I went inside she was on the backside of our house. After approximately five minutes I went out to bring them back inside. Tia was nowhere in sight. We had some trees taken down in the upper part of the yard and high weeds had started to grow in that area. I was so sure she had wandered up into them. I yelled for my husband who immediately came out. He said, "She has to be in the yard." He started looking one way as I went the other. I was limited in getting around because I was on a walker. When a dog goes missing, it is important not to panic.

Well, let me tell you, I failed that test. My mind became scattered. I called my son Jeff to come and help my husband look through the weeds. I frantically called my sister to start praying. I texted a real good friend, Debbie (who is an animal communicator), to see if she could connect with Tia. I knew I had to call Kayla, my granddaughter, to let her know what had happened. I was sobbing uncontrollably when she answered. It amazes me how she quickly took the adult role, trying to give me comfort. There was no way she could assist because she did not live in the area. By this time my sister and husband had arrived and started searching as well. Jeff was now cutting down weeds and shrubs in the yard with the hope of finding her. I then took to social media to ask for more prayers and to alert people to the fact that she was missing. My friend Bonnie arrived to help. We looked all over the yard and it was determined she must have been picked up by a bird of prey because there was no way she could have gotten out of the yard on her own, with it being completely fenced in. I found myself in a helpless situation. My mind took over. Did the bird drop her? Was she hurt and lying somewhere, unable to get back? It was about that time that Debbie texted me back. She told me Tia was out of the yard; she had pushed herself through a small opening under the fence and couldn't find her way back. She was somewhere in a grassy area.

Everyone started looking around the circumference of the house on both sides. We were now joined by Kelli, my daughter-in-law, and two grandchildren. It was starting to get dark. Bonnie went to the neighbor's yard to see if she had ventured over there. They also now joined the search. Still no Tia. It was like she had vanished. I was texting Debbie back and forth. She told me to calm down and she would encircle Tia with a light in the hopes that I would be able to locate her. I tried to remain calm, but fear was taking over. The neighbors up back came down with a four-wheeler to help light up parts of the woods behind our house. Calling her name was not really an option because she was so hard of hearing. I had my husband take my other two dogs (Chloe and Star) down on the road hoping she would hear them and it would bring her out. Unfortunately it did not. We took used clothing and put it outside our house along with her bed and a bowl of water. My plans were to sit on the porch all night until she found her way back.

I sat quietly on the bench in the front yard and Bonnie joined me. I thought I saw a light across the street and asked Bonnie to check it out. Tia was not there. By this time, the group decided it was too dark and dangerous to continue the search. It was decided that everyone would re-group first thing in the morning to continue the search for Tia. The night seemed like it would never end.

The next morning Bonnie and Donna (a very good friend, who watches my dogs when I'm away) arrived around 8:30 am. They were joined by family members and friends to map out a plan. Bonnie immediately started making flyers. I started calling shelters, rescues, and veterinarians. I received a text from Debbie stating that Tia had wandered further from home. When the flyers were done, Bonnie and Donna started going door to door handing them out. Another good friend, Becky, called stating she was coming over to help. When Bonnie gave a flyer to the neighbor who lives two doors down, the woman told Bonnie she saw Tia crossing the road at approximately 6:15 the night before. This confirmed she was out of the yard and that the search would focus across the street from our house. Everyone gathered and teams went in different directions. The brush was so heavy it was hard to get through. Also being so very small and black she could have been under a bush and passed over.

I sat waiting and praying. Calls were coming in along with Facebook messages with tons of prayers and many suggestions on how to possibly find your lost pet. I continued calling pet hospitals, shelters, and rescues. It amazed me how many there were to call. Just trying to stay focused was difficult. I had Becky contact Donna Crum, a good friend and animal cruelty officer for the area, to call a rescue group hoping they could work miracles. Unfortunately no one called back. I, too, called with no response. I received a call from Chris (a friend from Virginia) who suggested I contact Pure Gold Trackers.

Marsha (another good friend from Virginia) contacted me for a list of additional places with the hopes of finding her. This was becoming a nightmare from hell. How could this be happening to me? My baby was missing and I was helpless.

As evening approached my sister-in-law came up and suggested calling Roseann Turek, a local medium. I sent a private message asking her if she had any experience with finding lost dogs. She asked for a picture and before I could send it to her, she texted me back stating it was a little black dog. She started suggesting an area in which to look but it was very confusing. Around 9:30 pm, I asked if she was willing to come here and help. When she came, she led a group of six people on the search. She used energy and worked with a pendulum. They walked down a block and made a left. They walked down another block and stopped at a driveway on the right. She was sure that Tia was in that area. As I waited at home, I was certain that they would be bringing Tia home. My cell phone rang at about 10:30 asking if someone could bring me down to that area. When I arrived we continued looking. Because I was on a walker I was very limited as to how much I could do. After about an hour of searching, my son David came to me stating it was not safe to be walking around in the woods. We decided we would regroup the following morning.

My heart was broken. Where was Tia? Was she scared? Would our prayers be answered? I retired that night picturing her being covered by an angel's wings. I knew God would protect her.

The next morning we were up very early and were joined by additional friends: Teddy, Julie, Becky, Debbie and her husband Jim. Again the area was combed hoping Tia would be found. Jeff, David, and Randy looked in different areas. Roseann came back re-searching where she had been the night before. I reconnected with Debbie, the animal communicator, and she stated that Tia had been picked up and taken further away, possibly to a shelter. She researched more pet sites and sent them to me so I could list Tia as missing. I called our local shelter again to see if they could offer more assistance. Additional neighbors were on foot and in golf carts looking for any sign of her. Everyone was so supportive, but I was a mess! A neighbor who was out looking contacted a friend who is a medium from another area. He felt Tia was with a lady, he also stated there was a grey shed in her yard. My husband started riding around seeing if he could piece together what had been said. I re-called Roseann who sent me a map of another location where Tia possibly could be. We immediately went down to that area. We found nothing.

It was Monday, August 3rd and it felt like an eternity. Donna came down and drove me around the development. We stopped and talked to everyone we saw making them aware of Tia missing. Randy continued to put up more signs. He also took them to local gas stations, banks, post offices, grocery stores— anywhere people could see her picture to know we were looking for her. Next Donna and I went to recheck the bed we placed at the back of the house across the street. This was the direction the neighbor reported seeing Tia go. While we were there we heard some strange sounds, which Randy went to check on. Still, we could not find anything. By this time prank calls started coming in. They stated that they had her. People can be very cruel and sick, preying on the weakness of those in desperate need to find their pets.

I then contacted Sam Connelly, from Pure Gold Trackers to help. Many of my Rockville, Maryland friends highly recommended her. She stated she would get back to me that night with more information. Her website showed that she had had a lot of success but that sometimes the outcome is not as what would be hoped for. Still, the closure is so important. Sam got back to me stating she would not be able to come until Thursday, which meant waiting two more days. I had to stay strong so I scheduled the meeting. Tuesday morning I received a text to contact Bellabon Rescue, which I did. The woman started telling me to do all that I had already been doing. After we talked, as fate would have it, she was having Pure Gold Trackers come to assist her with a rescue. She then confirmed how she relied on them often.

I then received a text from Marsha from Virginia offering to help with calls. I texted her several resources: rescues, vets, and shelters. She also suggested I join a local neighborhood group known as Next Door. The next day I called Chris Bellevard only to find out that she was a friend of Sam Connelly! I asked her to give Sam a call and let her know of our connection. More flyers were made and hung, and Donna and I continued driving around the development.

In taking a break I got a surprise call from Sam Connelly stating the dog that she was called in to assist with the rescue had been found and she would be able to come that evening instead of Thursday. If she left at noon she could be at my house by 7 or 8 pm. She said in preparation for her arrival I needed to create a special flyer to be handed out to all neighbors. It stated: "FYI – The Pure Gold Trackers will be in the area this evening approximately 7pm. They will be utilizing a dog in the tracking process, looking for Tia the lost Dachshund. If you have window wells on your home, we ask that you please check inside the well. Please pray we find her tonight." Bonnie created the flyers and again she and Donna set out to deliver one to each neighbor. Sam arrived around 7:30 with Brie, her Golden tracking dog. Jeff was waiting to accompany her into the area across the road from our house.

Before they left, she made me aware that the search could end in three different ways. First, they would bring Tia back. Second, they would be bringing back her body, or third, Brie would lie down where her scent would have ended meaning that Tia had been picked up by someone or a predator. As they left in the pounding rain, we continued sitting on the porch watching and waiting. We could see the lights moving back and forth as they followed her trail. After about two hours, they came back to regroup and to give Brie a break. When they set back out Brie led them down the street exactly to where we were led by Roseann on Saturday night. This time Brie entered the driveway, then came back out and laid down on the side of the road. She was then asked to get back up and start tracking again but after doing it a second time she did the same thing, indicating the scent ended there and Tia had been picked up. They then came back to the house; oh I was so very sure they would have had Tia with them. We were approaching day six without her.

I reconnected with Debbie to see if she had had any communication with Tia. She told me her communication with her was very confusing. Tia told Debbie that she was not in a house, not in the woods, not in the grass. Debbie felt she may have passed, but said not to give up; "There is always hope." I contacted Roseann the medium to tell her the results of the tracking dog. She told me Tia had helped her. A bit confused I asked why. She stated she had been working in Psychic Investigation for five years and she knew she was closer to helping others in this unique way.

Friends continued to come by to help. Some continued to follow up with rescues, vets, and shelters. The list of calls was overwhelming. I was so thankful for their help! My circle of supporters was growing and I was getting calls from more and more people wanting to help find Tia. Until then, I did not know there were so many organizations to help. Some teams actually go out and spend hour after hour setting up feeding stations, humane traps and more. Because we only had the one sighting the night she went missing I had a hard time getting this to happen. I did, however, join numerous social media groups. I was directed to an organization known as Critter Cops. It is a one-of-a-kind service available in the US and Canada. I sent them Tia's info. They have a group of 130 people search the web, competing to find a match. They search all websites of pets that have been found resembling the pet's description. The first team member is paid a large bonus by Critter Cops, upon finding a confirmed match. They have thirty days to confirm a match before the bonus is no longer available. This definitely gave me some hope. So for a fee, I joined too. They were very supportive. I felt the more people I had working on getting Tia back, the better.

Days were passing, and all I could do was think of Tia. My baby was missing and I needed her back home to make my family whole again. Where was she? Was she safe? Was she with someone? I was approaching nine days without her; I was consumed with her. I received a text message that I should visit the local shelter where I had done training classes. Upon my arrival, the local television station was doing a short broadcast on the dogs needing forever homes. I asked a man named Tom, the shelter manager, if he felt they could do a brief caption on Tia. When he asked the reporter, he said he didn't think it would be permitted but that he would run it by his supervisor. God was on my side because an exception was made and within minutes I was being interviewed. I was then asked to forward a few of Tia's recent pictures that would be included with the caption, stating that she was missing and that help was needed to locate her. Everything would be run that night. I regained some hope. No way could that have been a coincidence that I received the text to go up to the shelter, finding the reporter there and the exception being made. I just knew she would be found!

I eventually received calls from people who saw the clip expressing their concern and willingness to help. Unfortunately, no Tia.

Then another longtime friend, Susie, called saying she contacted the local newspaper and a reporter would be reaching out to me for Tia's information so they could run a story on her. The amazing part of this was another exception was being made. They normally would not run this type of story in their paper. There were so many things happening in my favor, I just knew she was going to be found! She was getting so many prayers and I was meeting caring people from all parts of the world. There was no way she wouldn't return home soon.

What else could I do? I called a spiritual friend asking her if there was anything she would suggest. She told me she would join me in prayers for guidance. She told me she felt Tia was with St. Francis. I wanted to believe he would be with her but I was not ready to believe she was no longer alive. I would continue the search...

Tia had been gone for over two weeks, even though it seemed like forever. I would do a daily update on social media. More flyers were made that I took to a local printer to be printed. It was an option to have them printed on a type of paper that would not be ruined by the weather elements, which would only fade them over time. This seemed the best option to take. These were distributed to replace those that were ruined by all the recent rains. We also took them to local businesses. Keeping busy seemed to help me stay calm. Early morning and late evening were the worst times for me.

Our local newspaper was delivered by Cyndi. I asked her if I had mini flyers created would it be possible to have them inserted into the paper that would be delivered to all the homes in our development. This was now the next project at hand. Papers were stuffed and delivered to over 200 homes. With so much being done, why hadn't someone come forward to say they saw her, had her, or had tried to help her and she didn't make it? Even though the last possibility would be unbearable for me, at least I would have closure.

I never thought I would be dealing with Tia being missing. She was out there somewhere. But where? The pain, the sleepless nights, and not being able to eat or even function was something I never wanted anyone else to have to go through.

I started looking up inspirational quotes. The ones that really helped me cope dealt with believing, having faith, and never giving up. I knew deep down God had a plan. He was in control and I prayed daily asking Him to guide me, open my heart, and lead me to what was being asked of me to do. At that point it came to me. I could create a program in my neighborhood to help pets that may become lost to find their way home. I attended a meeting to propose my idea to the association. I told them I would send out letters to every home and lot owner explaining the program. I would have them register all the pets in their household. It would consist of the name, breed of cat or dog, color, and age. They would send me their information by text, mail, or phone. I would then create a spreadsheet. If a pet was found or lost I would be contacted in which case I would then create an Amber Alert and send it out. With everyone's help, we would strive to reunite pets with their owners in a timely manner. The program was to be called "For the Love of Tia". I would be in total charge with the intention being that the association would not have to add to their already-busy schedule. I am happy to say it was well received. Over 215 letters were prepared and sent out and within a matter of a few days there were over fifty pets registered.

Friends and family were very supportive. I had calls from people I didn't even know! Lisa B, Jackie, and Lisa F to name a few, would soon become lifelong friends. One suggested I contact Lost My Doggie, a program for missing dogs that creates flyers to be posted on social media. One part of their program specifically caught my eye. For a fee, they would issue an Amber Alert to 500 homes within a four-mile radius of where Tia was last seen. My thought was just how many people are on social media and may have seen her or even have her in their possession. Once the information was given to them, they put together a robocall that went out to all landline phones. A list was then sent to me as to who they called and what message they left. Even though I didn't get a lot of responses, something else was being done to try to find Tia. At this point in time, this is what mattered the most to me.

In the past whenever one of my dogs had become very ill and I had to make that dreaded decision it was heart-wrenching. But I at least had the chance to say goodbye, knowing they were going to be with God.

In 2017 my sheltie, Mickey, passed. He had been brought into our home when he was ten months old. Initially he was bred to be a show dog, but because of some minor issues, he did not qualify to meet their standards. In bringing him home I knew he was to have a different path. I was so right. In the twelve years I had him, he became a therapy dog. He received his certificate of achievement in which he had over fifty visits to nursing homes and schools. He accompanied me to all my trainings, so I could pursue my dog training career. He touched the lives of hundreds of people. When he left for Rainbow Bridge, I was awakened by the song "You Raised Me Up" by Josh Groban and I knew his goal was complete.

Then in 2019, I again had to say goodbye to Maggie. She was a little Chihuahua seven or eight years old who had a lot of issues, one being a fear-biter. After working to help her gain trust, she came to live with us for eight years, dying in my arms when she was sixteen. Again, after her passing, I was visited by the song, "Carrying Your Love With Me" by George Strait. I felt this was

Maggie's way of letting me know she was all right and that she loved me. Neither of these songs would I normally listen to, but I will never forget their message.

Then Tia went missing. No song came to me. Did this mean she was not okay? Possibly she was not able to come through. I sat quietly upstairs in the bedroom and concentrated deeply. Then the song, "Where Are You Christmas" by Faith Hill came to me. It was August. I wasn't listening to Christmas songs but how very fitting! My granddaughter, Kayla (who we got Tia for) sang this as a solo in her high school chorus many years before. In listening to the words in my head I kept hearing, "If you have love in your heart and your mind you will feel like Christmas all the time." I then knew even though she was not in sight, I would carry Tia in my heart forever.

I had to try and pull myself together. I had two other dogs Chloe and Star whom I also loved. I knew they were suffering as much as I was and that my emotions were affecting them. I started reading Bible verses in the hope that they would help me understand why I was going through all of this. I started saying over and over: "All things are possible with God, I place my trust in you O God, and Faith is being sure of what we hope for and certain of what we DO NOT SEE." Miracles happen every day. I just needed to be patient; mine would come.

On August 25th while scrolling through Facebook, I came across a course that was being offered by James Van Praagh. It was being offered live online in a three-day workshop known as "Spiritual Animal Friends". He scheduled special Animal Communicator guests who gave talks on different experiences. All three guests were very interesting. After the first class, I emailed Samantha Khury, a Professional Pet Interpreter who is a well-known communicator from the west coast. I told her about Tia and she sent me part of her book on finding lost animals. Within this book it states that it's very important to keep the pet in the present tense, visualize the pet already being home in your presence. Make yourself visible by walking the neighborhood and talking to everyone you see. When you have done everything possible you need to give it up to God. This seemed like an easy task but as soon as I would give it to Him I found myself taking it back.

I attended the next two classes and after each presentation there was a time for questions. There were so many who had questions it was almost impossible to be called on. After the last session, James stated he would be taking a short break and would come back on to answer additional questions. Mine was entered into the system. To my surprise, I was called on but, for some reason, they could not hear me respond. Sheer panic set in, I was so close! I immediately typed in stating I was still on just could not be heard. Luckily they saw my text and unmuted me so I could ask my question.

I explained how Tia went missing and everything I did to find her. Well not all that I did, that would have taken hours. James told me Tia was taken over a body of water and stated he felt Samantha Kuhry would be best to assist me. I told him I was in contact with Samantha by email. He then told me to call her direct and had his assistants give me her phone number. He told me that when she answered to tell her that he directed me to call.

It was going on 10:30 pm and I thought it would be too late to call her. Then I remembered she was on the west coast and that the time was earlier there. I couldn't wait to place the call. After a few rings, she answered. She told me she felt Tia was within a ¼ mile of our home. She told me, as stated in the book she sent me, to continue to keep Tia in the present tense and to make myself visible to anyone I came in contact with. I was to visualize Tia being home with me. She also told me to express gratitude to whoever had her and was taking care of her. She told me she would also continue to pray for her to be safely back in my arms.

The next day I could not wait to go to our local print shop and have more small photos of her printed. I was on a mission. My foot had healed and I was now able to drive and walk. My goal was to visit every single household in our development. Living rurally, the houses are spread out but I would take each section and canvas until I talked to everyone. After living here 32 years, I could not believe all the neighbors I had never met! As I proceeded on my mission, each person seemed so attuned to my desire to bring Tia home. Everyone was so willing to keep an eye out and to call me if they had any information. One person stated her husband had a printing shop and was willing to help with additional flyers if needed. In addition to talking to people regarding Tia, I took down information to add to the program I recently started, "For the Love of Tia". We talked about the importance of everyone being alerted

when a pet is found or lost. And most of
all, never assume it can't happen to
them.

Canvasing the development took me
four days. It was time to wait and pray
that someone would find her. While
waiting another idea came to me. The
signs that people put into the ground at
election time seemed to be another
visual I could use. I contacted friends
who had them and asked if they would
be willing to give them to me. My
husband spray painted them black and
we then stapled one of Tia's posters to
each side. Above the poster I painted in
big white letters, "LOST DOG".

Next, my husband and I went around
our development putting the signs in
highly visible areas. I called a few
neighbors outside of the development
within a two-mile range and asked if
they would allow me to put them on

their property. Everyone was more than willing to do this for me. A neighbor who lived down the street that I had never met, came to my door and expressed how deeply saddened she was that Tia was still not home. She asked if I had any signs left, for she would like to display one in front of her house too.

We were fast approaching the end of September. I was surfing Facebook and couldn't believe what I was reading and seeing. Someone from a nearby town had posted a picture of a dachshund that looked a lot like Tia. It said she got out of their home and was missing. Was this her? Was it possible that she was picked up by someone thinking she was a stray? Someone who was giving her a good home? Did she get away and was trying to find her way back home to me? As fast as I saw the post, it was taken down. I remembered Wendy was the one who reposted it for someone. I immediately contacted Wendy who then contacted her friend to get more information. No one seemed to know where the original post came from. The only thing they could relay is that the dog was found and that it was deceased. The emotional roller coaster was taking over: what if it was Tia? Unless I could see the dog, I would not know for sure. If it was her, she needed to be given a proper farewell. Answers were not to be found. This went on until the next day at around four in the afternoon when I finally found out that the dog was definitely not Tia. The dog belonged to a caring family for many years. They had carpenters working on their house that left the gate open and the dog named Princess got out. She was deaf and blind and wandered into a nearby pond and drowned. My heart ached for them. I was relieved it was not Tia but again I had no closure.

The months were passing. It was the beginning of October. The days were getting shorter and the nights were cooler. Again I revisited all I had done to find her. I continued to read scripture and to journalize many quotes of encouragement. I can honestly say this is what kept me sane. My husband and I were invited to an anniversary party. I read somewhere that there are no coincidences. Coincidences are God's gift while remaining anonymous. God knew just how much I was struggling. We were sitting at a table with an extra seat. Father Jim, a very good friend, sat down beside me. He recently had to say goodbye to his dog, Star.

Father Jim was definitely an animal lover and we began to share many stories about how much joy they bring to us. I told him how I was hurting inside and just couldn't seem to move forward or think about anything else. He told me he understood and explained that I should write down all that had been done to try and bring Tia home. He said visibly seeing the list makes the effort more real. I also expressed my concern about it getting dark outside. For some reason that was a real issue I was dealing with. He told me he was going to give me a blessed candle that would burn for about four days. I was to light it and place it somewhere outside where I could see it. Father Jim actually put the candle in my hands later that day. I knew the perfect place to put it. In the upper part of my yard is a statue of Saint Padre Pio. I have had many amazing miracles happen through his intercession. It is about 100 feet from our sunroom. I immediately placed it in the stones at the front of the statue. It would remain there day and night until Tia was found. I had a small table that I could put over the candle to protect it from the weather elements.

Knowing the candle from Father Jim would burn for about four days, I contacted Judy, a member of our church, to see if I could purchase blessed candles to replace them as soon as the flame went out.

Looking up the yard each night and seeing that flame burning gave me hope. Knowing the flame was burning, represented warmth and light around Tia and would continue to burn until I knew where she was. I read the passage "Where there is Hope, there is Faith. Where there is Faith, Miracles Happen." Everyone was praying for a miracle and I knew God would not let me down. I had to be patient. Everything would work out as planned.

Being a dog trainer and seeing my clients was definitely keeping me busy and helped me to focus on something over which I had control. I was scheduled to see my first client on November 5th. She was not too far from my home. As I was getting ready, I received a call from her stating she had to reschedule. I found myself dreading the thought of my day turning into one of self-pity.

My husband and I were sitting at the kitchen table having coffee when I thought I saw something at the kitchen window.

On second glance I realized it was a woodpecker. I had heard before that birds will see their reflection in a window but this one was different. He left and came back, then sat on the window ledge and pecked at the casing around the window. This went on for about twenty minutes. I took numerous pictures of him and also a video. He then left the kitchen window and went to the side window and then to the front window, where Tia and Chloe would sit on the couch looking out. I became so occupied with this bird I didn't realize he had entertained me for over an hour.

When he finally left, I was intrigued to find out the meaning of a woodpecker's visit. In looking it up I learned that it was time to pay attention because an opportunity had come knocking along with it. In other words, the woodpecker signals to you that significant changes are happening in your life. Therefore, it is up to you to seize the moment. This had to be a sign! What was going to happen? My mind started racing. Were my prayers and those of everyone else finally going to be answered? Please God, I asked. Please help me to see what's ahead of me.

My dogs Chloe and Star were being affected by my emotions. Chloe was dealing with stomach issues and Star, only a baby himself, seemed to be moping around. As the days passed I knew we needed to focus on their well-being too. My husband and I started to discuss the possibility of bringing another puppy into the mix. Chloe was twelve years old and I definitely wanted her around to help train the new little one.

Later that day I remembered a dachshund breeder who had called me for help in understanding Tellington TTouch (a technique that is part of my dog training). She had felt with better knowledge that she could incorporate it into her breeding profession, so I decided to look up her information. I could not believe what I was seeing! The one and only day I had connected with Bonnie was three years prior on November 6th. Now I was reaching out to her again on the very same day of the year, explaining how my precious Tia was lost. I sought to find out if there was something I was missing in trying to find her. Unfortunately she had nothing to add regarding that. She told me she was still breeding and that her focus was on the long-haired dachshunds now instead of the smooth coated ones. A litter had just been born and all were promised loving homes. She would not be breeding again until the following year, but she would send me information regarding her puppies, which came from champion lines. Later that day an email arrived with pictures, information, and pricing. After reviewing everything, I was very impressed but it would have to be a future decision as no puppies were then available.

"When the time is right I will make it happen," Isaiah 60:22.

Two days after talking to Bonnie she called me back. She stated that one of the promised puppies that was born on November 4th apparently was born without a front paw. The puppy would not be going to the prospective new home after all. She told me other than the missing paw the pup appeared in good health and was wondering if I was interested in giving her a good home. She stated she was not sure what she would need cost-wise in the future so the pup would be given to me cost-free. After talking awhile Bonnie stated that she knew it was a big decision for me and that I could get back to her later. It was not something that needed an immediate answer.

My thoughts were running rampant. I was still searching for Tia. When found, would her medical needs be increased? Would my other two dogs accept a new puppy? Would they be too much for a puppy without a front paw? Most of all, was I ready to take on the challenge of a new puppy with a birth defect?

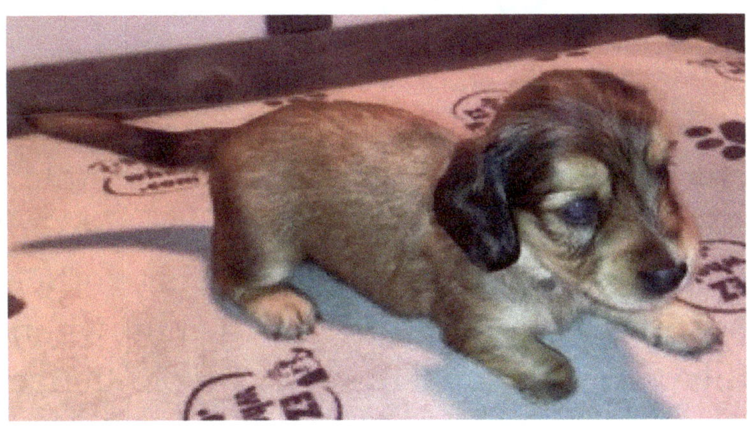

I began to pray even more for direction. My husband and I discussed the pros and cons and after much consideration decided there was a definite reason she was being offered to me. I just needed to have faith.

I called Bonnie back that evening and told her I was definitely interested and I told her I wanted the pup's name to be Faith. She needed to start calling her that whenever she would be with her. Bonnie sent me the pictures. Faith was adorable and very active.

I had to believe this was the significant change that the woodpecker foretold. Was Faith being sent to me not only to help me but to help comfort other people also going through turmoil when their pets are missing? I had confidence that the answer would come in time.

I still continued to check Lost and Found pages. From time to time, I would get a text message or a call directing me to go to a specific page to see if that was Tia. So many resembled her. If only I had had her chipped it would've been so much easier to identify her, but at the time she was a puppy this was not a common practice.

As time passed, I knew she would definitely have a different appearance. She probably would be much grayer and thinner. Then all of a sudden a dachshund appeared; it was Tia! She was found as a stray in North Carolina! Someone posted her picture, stating they had found the dog on their property. We were talking many miles away but I had often read of how dogs are picked up and dropped off in different states. She looked weather-beaten. All I knew is that I needed to connect with those who had her and get her back into my arms.

When I put the call into the number on the site, I got an answering machine. My heart was pounding waiting for the return call. In revisiting the page it stated she was being picked up by a local rescue. Please, please call me back before I lose touch with where she is going! My cell phone rang. A very nice lady on the other end stated she had just picked her up. I tearfully explained how Tia had gone missing and that I had been looking for her for months. I was so sure it was her. We started comparing each dog, both were spayed, possibly fifteen years or older. This was definitely a senior dog who seemed hard of hearing. She asked if I could send her recent pictures to confirm the match. She also said a transport would have to be put into place and that I would be responsible for the vet bills. This definitely was not going to be a problem! I told her I actually never dropped Tia's insurance. At the time it seemed to be a way of holding onto the vision of her coming home.

After the lady received the pictures I sent in a text, she called me and certain features stood out. She took pictures of the dog she had and texted them to me. This dog definitely had more brown on her feet. Tia's were almost gray. Even though this pup seemed to be a senior, after seeing pictures of her teeth, they were much whiter than Tia's. My heart was broken once again.

At this point, we were both crying. I told her how grateful I was for all she was doing in her rescue efforts. She told me she was almost as convinced as I was that Tia had been found. Then she told me that they often give strays a name. She asked if I would have a problem if she called her Tia. I was honored and even though it was not my Tia, my faith was stronger that miracles do happen.

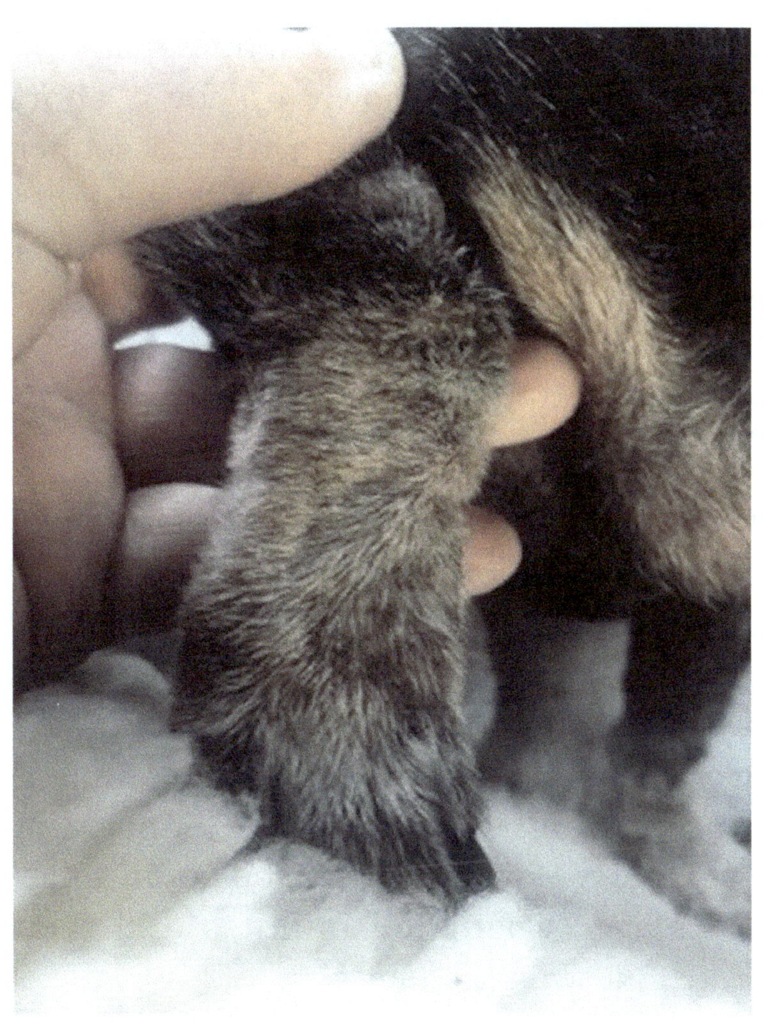

Surrounding myself with movies of hope, faith, and miracles kept me being positive. When I came home from work two weeks later, my husband said the woodpecker had shown up for a short visit but didn't stay long. He no sooner was telling me about it when it made its presence known. I guess to make sure I was on the right track. I will admit it was not easy.

Another two weeks passed. While we were sitting in the front room watching TV, we suddenly heard a strange noise. At first we could not determine from where it was coming. Our front door has a window panel on each side. The sound was coming from that direction. The woodpecker was back but this time it was looking in the window panel and knocking. Boy, did I wish he could talk! He stayed about ten minutes and then left. That was his last visit.

Would a Christmas miracle happen? A woman from my church called and told me she had been praying for me, for Tia's return. She told me for some reason the name Fritz kept coming to her and was wondering if I knew anyone with that name. After much thought, the only thing I could come up with was Fritz as a nickname for Francis. Possibly it was God's way of telling me Tia was with St. Francis? She also asked if she could create an updated poster. The top would read: "Looking for a Christmas miracle". I would then be able to revisit areas and let everyone know how Tia was still missing and that we were praying for a miracle. My heartfelt gratitude went out to her.

Then it came to me, that when a dog becomes lost, they are really not lost at all; they become a guide. They lead you on a journey. You meet people from all parts of the world. You reacquaint with old friends. They bring out the goodness in people and mend old wounds. When you are open to this, everything fits into God's design and purpose. "Live by faith, not by sight." Romans 8:28. I was seeing that all of this had a purpose.

Was it now time to help others? Dogs go missing every day. I could now relate to owner's fears and anxieties. Someone from a local town heard about Tia and she called me in despair. She stated that her little dachshund had been taken outside by her husband in the evening as he always did and the dog seemed to vanish. She was very upset. I could tell her what I did and told her to never give up. After talking with her for quite a while I asked her what the dog's name was; I would keep her and the pup in my prayers. She stated his name was "Peanut". That actually was my brother's nickname, my brother who passed away a few years before. Again God's way of remaining anonymous why telling me to keep believing.

It was time to go meet Faith. She was adorable and so very tiny. Bonnie told me she was getting around just fine and already responding to her name. We spent some time enjoying this sweet little angel. Bonnie's rule was to never to allow a puppy to go to its new home before eight weeks of age. We talked about what would be best for her. She felt that the other puppies in the litter could start to overpower her and, with only having the three paws, coming to live with me at seven weeks might be for the better. In looking at the calendar that would make the transition to our home December 22nd or 23rd. As we were leaving she told me she would be sending me pictures and videos so that I could watch Faith's progress.

December 17th brought a huge snowstorm. As you might remember I had been making sure the candle up the yard by St Padre Pio stayed lit. In waking that morning and seeing the amount of snow we received, in my mind there was absolutely no way that candle could still be burning. The snow was about three feet deep. I had to

make my way up to my St. Padre Pio
statue and the candle. So, shovel in
hand, I began my quest. It was not easy
because of how deep it was. After a few
breaks I finally arrived at the statue.
The table over the candle was
completely covered with snow. I started
removing all the snow and to my
amazement, the candle was still
burning! How was this possible? Again
a miracle.

The day was approaching to bring little
Faith home. I thought of how she would
be changing my life. I was sure she was
a gift from God and that there was a

plan already in place. I reflected on all that had happened within the last five months, including the program I had started to reunite lost pets. I have since started a Private Facebook group to encourage prayers for the owners of lost pets and for those who spend numerous hours in their search to bring pets safely home.

I'm sure our journey together has just begun. This little puppy has a very big job to do! She came to live with us December 23rd, 2020. Tia was born on December 22nd, 2008.

You have read my story. I am still looking for Tia. I'm sure that it is something I will do forever, but it's so important to know that all things are possible with God. You have read how Tia has helped me grow in faith. Two weeks before FAITH came to live with us, my thoughts came to a halt when I realized that if you take the F and the H off of her name and reverse the middle it is TIA spelled backward.

Coincidence???? I don't think so.....

Message from the Author

I started in the K-9 training profession in 2008 and graduated from Animal Behavior College as a Certified Dog Trainer working with obedience and behavior issues. Training consists of 100% positive reinforcement and behavior modification. In 2011 I recognized that dogs that are imbalanced emotionally, physically and mentally show signs of fear, preventing them from being able to think and learn.

I then became part of the **Tellington TTouch** Program. After finishing 3 years of training in Rockville, Maryland I became a certified Tellington TTouch Practitioner. TTouch is changing the behavior of an animal by the touch of your hand, doing ground work and using training equipment. This helps reduce fear and builds trust which allows the animal to think and learn.

I am a member of Pet Professional Guild, Tellington TTouch Guild, Mid Atlantic Association of Professional Positive Dog Trainers, Dogs Natural Elite and a former member of Therapy Dogs International.

As long as I can remember, my goal in life was to work with animals. I always instilled in my family that following your dreams is very important. All I needed was a gentle push from my granddaughter Kayla to realize it was time to take my own advice, and pursue

my lifelong dream. I am wife, mother
and grandmother and the owner of
Reese's Training of the Heart. I now
have two dogs, Star and Faith.

I invite you to learn more at
http://k9touchoftrust.com
Follow me on Facebook at
**https://www.facebook.com/Reeses-
Training-from-the-Heart**